One-Minute Prayers™

FOR THOSE WHO *Hurt*

Text by Hope Lyda

HARVEST HOUSE PUBLISHERS

EUGENE, OREGON

ONE-MINUTE PRAYERS is a series trademark of The Hawkins Children's LLC. Harvest House Publishers, Inc., is the exclusive licensee of the trademark ONE-MINUTE PRAYERS.

Cover by Garborg Design Works, Minneapolis, Minnesota

Cover photo © Getty Images

ONE-MINUTE PRAYERS™ FOR THOSE WHO HURT

Copyright © 2005 by Harvest House Publishers
Eugene, Oregon 97402

ISBN 0-7369-1558-3

Printed in the United States of America

05 06 07 08 09 10 11 12 / BP-KB / 10 9 8 7 6 5 4 3 2 1

Contents

Morning   5

Brokenness   7
Searching 13
Fragile 21
Patterns 27
Loneliness 33
Motion 39
Healing 45
Excuses 51
Protection 57
Love 63
Peace 69
Meaning 75
Reaching 81
Acceptance 87
Giving and Receiving 93
Wholeness 99
Perspective 105
Belief 111
Joy 117
Character 123
Discovery 129
Changing Course 135

Night 141

Facing Another Day

Let the morning bring me word of your unfailing love, for I have put my trust in you. Show me the way I should go, for to you I lift up my soul.

PSALM 143:8

This is the hardest part. I wake up and go to the window, hoping the landscape of my circumstance has varied. I watch for bluebirds and signs of forgotten flowers rising to greet the sun. But the land is barren. Reminders of a better day lie dormant against lattice and along the fence. That fence went up to define a good space. Now it is a reminder of limitations, boundaries, restrictions.

Let this day be something special, Lord, with one spark of joy, one ounce of relief, one bit of insight. I must measure my hopes in such ways, Lord. As with so many other people facing a rough journey, one day at a time is all I can pray about. Help me face this beginning with a bit more strength than the day before. This is my prayer.

Brokenness

The Rubble of Old Ways

*Like a city whose walls are broken down is a man
who lacks self-control.*

PROVERBS 25:28

I feel so vulnerable these days. My fortress of perceived togetherness and success has been destroyed. I step over the rubble that was once a supposedly good life and raise my hands to heaven. What now, Lord? What now?

I trust You to raise up what is truly an honorable, meaningful existence. Out of these ashes and the debris of broken dreams and an adjusted sense of happiness, I ask You to create something wonderful, something that reminds me what true love is.

After the Fall

The bows of the warriors are broken, but those who stumbled are armed with strength.

1 SAMUEL 2:4

Lord, You have made the weak strong. Your power rushes through my veins as I struggle to stand and face the fight of my trial. There are many mighty warriors about me who seem to manage their way fine. But I have taken a fall. All that I have worked hard for crumbles to the ground.

Yet, I also know what it is like to fall into Your strength—to surrender my will to Your own, to know that there is a good thing taking shape that I cannot see right now. You cover me with strength and ability. You will carry me through the days ahead.

Mending the Break

You will say then, "Branches were broken off so that I could be grafted in." Granted. But they were broken off because of unbelief, and you stand by faith. Do not be arrogant, but be afraid.

ROMANS 11:19-20

I make room for You in the most indirect ways. Instead of inviting You into my life, Lord, and asking You to rule over it with Your love and mercy, I force the situation. I fail, I stumble, I break off branches of my life, and then look to You to fix these pieces and make them stronger. I ask You to mend me so that I may bear the fruit of righteousness.

I cannot take credit for the times I do rise above such humbling circumstances. It is Your doing. I pray to be able to start trusting You from the beginning, to not require so much mending. I invite You to extend my branches to reach out in new ways. I stand by faith.

Weak Are Made Strong

But we have this treasure in jars of clay to show that this all-surpassing power is from God and not from us.

2 CORINTHIANS 4:7

Anyone who knows the past problems in my life is amazed at how You continue to use me...a very broken, weak vessel. I am not whole in the way the world expects, but I am made whole, strong, and redeemable by Your grace. The cracks that other people see only increase the praise and credit I can offer You.

To those who wonder I can say, "See this missing piece? See this shattered bit of pottery? My Potter is still able to fill me with His purpose and call me a worthy vessel." As I speak these words and pray this praise, I thank You, Lord, for calling me beautiful. I am a treasure that desires to be filled again and again.

Searching

On a Quest

*So I turned my mind to understand, to investigate
and to search out wisdom and the scheme of things
and to understand the stupidity of wickedness and
the madness of folly.*

ECCLESIASTES 7:25

I am on a quest for knowledge, Lord. Something good that has come from my recent time of desperation and depletion is that I am hungry to understand and gather wisdom about how life works. Help me to see how my former ways might have complicated Your plan for my life. I do not want to dwell on these errors. You have forgiven them. But I do want to learn from my folly and my impatient days.

Give me a heart for what is true, holy wisdom. Guide my actions and thoughts so that I take this new knowledge and pull it into the way I live. I see this quest as an eternal thing. I no longer will be in a hurry to learn the lessons You have for me, Lord.

Learning to Ask

Ask and it will be given to you; seek and you will find; knock and the door will be opened to you.

MATTHEW 7:7

I am beginning to understand the whole asking thing. I come to You, prayerful and in need of so many things that I struggle to know where and how to begin. But my heart is leading the way, not my covetous, human spirit. I ask You today for comfort. There...I said it. I am hurt. I worry. I doubt those parts of me that used to seem like absolutes, like my faith, my hope in a future, and my ability to hear You.

I need You greatly, deeply, and now. I am standing at the door of my future and knocking. I no longer make demands while peeking through the keyhole. I wait till the door is wide open. I see Your compassion, and I fall to my knees. I am thankful You have opened up Your love to me.

Right Heart

When you ask, you do not receive, because you ask with wrong motives, that you may spend what you get on your pleasures.

JAMES 4:3

I do not doubt that when I ask for things lately, I am asking with wrong motives. I am calling on Your power to transform my weak attempts or selfish inquiries into requests that are worthy of You. I am overwhelmed and have lost my ability to connect with most people around me. So when I come to You in that haze that defines me right now, I pray for Your grace.

You know my heart. Its motives are good. You see through all that is not me, and reclaim for my future the real me...the me You created to have a right heart for You.

Encouraging Words

Stop doing wrong, learn to do right! Seek justice, encourage the oppressed.

ISAIAH 1:16-17

I keep telling myself to do better, to push through this moment in my life. Will I recall ten years from now how hard this year was? I know I will remember the small kindnesses expressed by other people. My visual memories will be of the places I have visited and the faces that have appeared along my journey. I may not recall names, but I know that many impressions have been made on my heart.

Lord, encourage my spirit. When I am tempted to focus on my failings or missed opportunities, remind me that I am precious in Your sight. I am learning to do right by myself and by You.

Figuring Out the Season

There is a time for everything,
and a season for every activity under heaven:

a time to be born and a time to die,
a time to plant and a time to uproot,
a time to kill and a time to heal,
a time to tear down and a time to build,
a time to weep and a time to laugh,
a time to mourn and a time to dance,
a time to scatter stones and a time to gather them,
a time to embrace and a time to refrain,
a time to search and a time to give up,
a time to keep and a time to throw away,
a time to tear and a time to mend,
a time to be silent and a time to speak,
a time to love and a time to hate,
a time for war and a time for peace.

ECCLESIASTES 3:1-8

Lord, I pray to understand what season I am in now. Reveal to me what this time is about in my life. Guide me toward the lessons I should take hold of. Stop me from making this time into a season that is not of You. Let this time of difficulty give way to a time of celebration and peace. I search my future for the new season that will surely come.

Fragile

My Favorite Hiding Place

Rescue me from my enemies, O LORD, for I hide myself in you.

PSALM 143:9

If these current hurts can be my teachers, they offer me lessons about whom to trust and where to run. I cannot hide from life, though I have tried that during my weakest moments. But I can seek Your shelter when the most difficult enemies start to undermine my purpose. These enemies—fatigue, sorrow, doubt, fragility, stubbornness—seem insurmountable at times, until I can run to You.

Lord, You are my favorite hiding place. You offer a drink to cool me, a bed for rest, and protection against these threats to my life. Soon You will encourage me with words I need to hear. Then I will return to make my way through this circumstance, no longer weary, no longer fearful.

Walking the Valley

*Even though I walk through the valley of the shadow
of death, I will fear no evil, for you are with me;
your rod and your staff, they comfort me.*

PSALM 23:4

I am removed from those on the mountain. I look
up and wave or nod to them along their journey. But I
am here in the valley, Lord. This is where lush life
grows, but for me it is a time of sorrow and uncertainty.
I can only glance at those on higher plains once in a
while, because my time here is so burdensome. Each
step I take is my only focus.

But then up ahead I see You standing with Your rod
and staff. You are waiting patiently and pointing out the
secure places to step. I am almost there. Now we walk
together, and You point out a mountain in the future
that will be mine. Your promise to lead me out of the
valley, Lord, is my only focus.

Great Expectations

Watch and pray so that you will not fall into temptation. The spirit is willing, but the body is weak.

MATTHEW 26:41

Oh, I am so willing, Lord. My spirit craves to do right. My heart beats so that I may grow to love You more. I pray for my life today and in the days ahead. I know there will be many times when I am tempted to quit the journey, stop caring, fade from my life.

Your love for me is my lifeline during these times. My spirit can cling to You and see the way through simple, everyday circumstances and the most difficult situations. It all feels hard right now, so I will not trust my first physical reaction. I will only trust the pull of my spirit toward Your presence.

Handle with Care

Turn to me and be gracious to me, for I am lonely and afflicted.

PSALM 25:16

Turn to me, Lord. Look at my face. See beyond the eyes, the lines, the signs of fatigue. See through to me. You understand what will raise me from this time. I cannot figure it out, and other people do not know what I need.

Turn to me, Lord. Be gracious to me. My loneliness haunts me. My pain is real. I have nobody to explain it to, figure it out with, who will fully understand. So I keep it all: the loneliness, the pain, the worry. It lies down with me, and even my dreams do not provide distance.

Turn to me, Lord. Let me rest my weary mind and body and spirit in Your presence while You watch over me.

Patterns

Not That I Want to Know

How many wrongs and sins have I committed?
Show me my offense and my sin.

JOB 13:23

I do not really want to know, but I feel I should ask about the sin in my life, Lord. There are times I am so caught up in survival mode that my rationale is "anything that gets me through this is okay." Which leads me to believe I should probably be asking the question: What offenses am I committing?

My insecurities keep me pretty timid. I do not expect to hear of major sin in my life right now, but I am aware of the subtle ways I am working against Your will. My pride can refuse help. My anxiousness refuses rest. My stubborn streak resists change. These are the daily sins from which I need relief. I guess, Lord, I am asking You to save me from myself so that I can make room for all the provision You have for me.

Knowing the Way Home

Show me your ways, O LORD, teach me your paths;
guide me in your truth and teach me, for you are
God my Savior, and my hope is in you all day long.

PSALM 25:4-5

I have walked the roads back to myself and my old life so many times that I do it blindly, forgetting that You are taking me to a new place, along a new route. Forgive me for not rejoicing in this different journey. I had plans: people to see, things to do. I recognize that in hard times we learn great lessons that enrich our lives and our relationship with You. Even with this understanding, I am reluctant to follow at times.

So far, the scenery is not comforting. I must rely on You for everything: the map, the directions, safety along the way, and nourishment. No longer can I run to the places that used to be my refuge. This makes me anxious. Help me to place my hope in You, Lord. You do not guide me toward destruction, only toward resurrection from my old life. Give me faith to follow You home.

Blinded by Trouble

*Do not withhold your mercy from me, O LORD; may
your love and your truth always protect me. For
troubles without number surround me; my sins
have overtaken me, and I cannot see. They are
more than the hairs of my head, and my heart fails
within me.*

PSALM 40:11-12

The darkness of my struggle covers my eyes and my
heart. I reach out my hands to feel my way through the
mire. Troubles more numerous than the sands of Your
beaches and the hairs on my head come at me, and in
my blind state I have no response time. Lord, protect
me. Do not remove Your cover of mercy as I relearn
how to get through my days.

My heart beats slowly and without conviction. That
perhaps is the saddest part of my life right now. I am
overwhelmed by my old ways and old self. Release me
from the patterns that hold me hostage. Release me to
Your mercy.

What Comes from Faith

But someone will say, "You have faith; I have deeds." Show me your faith without deeds, and I will show you my faith by what I do.

JAMES 2:18

Lord, thank You for my steadfast faith in earlier times. Oh, how You protected me from becoming too lazy in my belief. I let go of some of Your precepts when life went smoothly, but I have never removed myself from Your love and covering. I have never doubted that the goodness I tasted came from Your provision.

Now, as goodness seems foreign, I continue to express my life in the way of faith. My deeds are the result of a deeply rooted faith in You and Your strength and Your existence. Had I not developed traditions of prayer, forgiveness, and community, I would be left without a dwindling hope. Thank You. Thank You for inspiring a spiritual life with rich dimension. It holds me up in this moment.

Loneliness

Never Alone

But a time is coming, and has come, when you will be scattered, each to his own home. You will leave me all alone. Yet I am not alone, for my Father is with me.

JOHN 16:32

Other people may come and go, leaving the life I know to go on to other things, but this is to be expected. Why, though, does this hurt me so? I take it personally that others are finding their foothold and stepping up or out, and You have called me to remain here alone, figuring it all out slowly and with much trepidation.

I know that I am not alone. I am never alone, for You are with me and You see where I stand. You see my sorrow and the loneliness that fills my days. I do not have a home to return to—not yet. But You prepare a place for me in this life and also in eternity. This is the future home I have to long for. This is the home that draws me back into the shelter of love and comfort.

Wisdom of the Widow

The widow who is really in need and left all alone puts her hope in God and continues night and day to pray and to ask God for help.

1 TIMOTHY 5:5

The loss of what is familiar to me leaves me feeling alone. God, You care for the most basic of my needs. I must trust You in the same way a widow does, as if my life depended on Your provision and mercy. This is truly a life of faith. When I felt strong and in control, I was losing sight of how to depend on You and Your help.

Night and day, I call out my needs to You and wait for them to be covered. The emptiness in me opens to the point of pain so that I can receive Your mercy. I am left alone with my thoughts and emotions, but I am never left alone in my need. Grant me the ability to firmly understand and praise You for this difference.

Free in Our Slavery

Though we are slaves, our God has not deserted us in our bondage. He has shown us kindness in the sight of the kings of Persia: He has granted us new life to rebuild the house of our God and repair its ruins, and he has given us a wall of protection in Judah and Jerusalem.

EZRA 9:9

My prison is becoming familiar to me. I fear I might become accustomed to this sense of restriction and poverty and never return to a life where I am totally free. God, be with me now and teach me the lessons of freedom that You offered slaves and captives—those who were mistreated, abused, and considered less than human.

The secret You offer is hope in the face of indifference, resurrection in the face of death, and peace in the face of hatred. You give a new life to those who seek Your face during their unfathomable moments in the pit of despair. You protect the most important part of me, Lord. You know it is my soul, my spirit that must rise above these circumstances. Through my spirit, I will forever be free.

Motion

Action

But Jesus immediately said to them: "Take courage! It is I. Don't be afraid." "Lord, if it's you," Peter replied, "tell me to come to you on the water." "Come," he said. Then Peter got down out of the boat, walked on the water and came toward Jesus.

MATTHEW 14:27-29

When You call us into action, Lord, it is for our own good. It is a way of moving us forward and toward a future. Because I am so weary, I long to sit. I fantasize about falling into a deep slumber and waking up once this struggle is over. But, Lord, You waken me to the wonder of trusting You.

Help me recognize Your face and Your voice as You call me to take action. What should I do, Lord? Ask it of me, and give me the strength…and the faith…to follow through.

Model Behavior

Whatever you have learned or received or heard from me, or seen in me—put it into practice. And the God of peace will be with you.

PHILIPPIANS 4:9

During this time, I have spent moments reflecting on the blessing of those people who model a strong Christian faith. I thank You for the gifts of friends, family members, and strangers who have shown me aspects of Your character. I draw on this heritage when I need to make decisions.

There are days when I am functioning on autopilot. God, I want to surrender my actions to Your will. I want to step out with a strong faith. When I do not know what to do, I will rely on what I have learned, received, and heard from those who have walked before me.

God Appears

Let us acknowledge the LORD; let us press on to acknowledge him. As surely as the sun rises, he will appear; he will come to us like the winter rains, like the spring rains that water the earth.

HOSEA 6:3

I am not aware of much these days. I pray to be perceptive of how You move through me and around me. I need these signs of Your activity in my life. Much escapes my attention. I am slow to catch what people are saying to me. It is only by Your grace that I get through the days.

While in this time of hibernation, I pray to be awakened to Your touch. May I notice it in the rising sun and the life-giving rains. These are not only symbols of hope, but are also evidence of Your active presence. This is a truth I so desperately need to hold on to.

Know When to Stand Firm

Therefore, my dear brothers, stand firm. Let nothing move you. Always give yourselves fully to the work of the Lord, because you know that your labor in the Lord is not in vain.

1 CORINTHIANS 15:58

I am making slow but sure progress toward my goals. I sense Your leading and have received wise counsel from people of faith. I am giving myself over to the work You have placed in front of me, and I am thankful for it. I realize that there are times You ask me to not move. You require me to be still and stand firm.

Having an unmoving faith means I must lean against the rock of Your salvation. I cling to its strength and know the form of its power so well. My ideas change and my opinions vary, but I do not move from my life's foundation.

Healing

The Process

Blessed are those who mourn, for they will be comforted.

MATTHEW 5:4

I am used to taking aspirin when my head aches. I drink fizzy beverages when my stomach hurts. But when my heart aches and my life is broken, I must face the spiritual process for healing. I must release myself to mourning. Lord, I can only do this because You are my Foundation.

I give myself over to Your comfort. Giving way to the flood of sorrow is not easy for me, Lord. I like to stay in control. You know all that needs healing in my life. Reach down and inspire my healing to begin.

Looking Ahead

*I know that my Redeemer lives, and that in the end
he will stand upon the earth.*

JOB 19:25

When I want explanations for my circumstances or
easy fixes for my ailing life, I know that I am requesting
unnecessary things. You do not call me to "get" everything about my troubles. You do call me to trust You. It
is not with reprimands or rules that You require this of
me. It is through Your love.

I cannot be certain how this time will play out. I do
not know the answers that will come my way, or if only
more questions will fill my mind. The vision of healing
I hope for might not come to pass. You might offer
something completely different for my life.

What I do know is that, at the very end, I will experience healing as I run to You—my Redeemer.

I Will

*Heal me, O LORD, and I will be healed; save me and
I will be saved, for you are the one I praise.*

JEREMIAH 17:14

I will ask to be healed, and I will be healed. I will
ask to be saved, and I will be saved. You are the One I
come to in my distress or frustration, because You are
with me in my times of fulfillment and contentment. So
I know You are with me now. Praising what You are
doing in my life feels awkward at times, because it
seems so far from a hopeful situation. Yet, I praise You
honestly and with belief that I am precious to You.

I will muster up the courage to ask, Lord. And I will
hear Your response of acceptance, love, and comfort.

Because It Is Done

*He said to me: "It is done. I am the Alpha and the
Omega, the Beginning and the End. To him who is
thirsty I will give to drink without cost from the
spring of the water of life."*

REVELATION 21:6

You started and finished all that needs to be done,
for now and for all time. There is nothing I need to
accomplish that will change or secure that. That is not
my job nor the purpose You have given to me. I am to
be in covenant with You, seeking Your presence and fol-
lowing in Your way so that I honor, accept, and give
glory to the Alpha and the Omega.

Because You have done all that is required, You offer
refreshment with the water of life. There is no need to
explain my thirst, because You know all that I experience. And as I drink to fill my need, I know there is no
cost because You already paid it.

Excuses

Forgive

Bear with each other and forgive whatever grievances you may have against one another. Forgive as the Lord forgave you.

COLOSSIANS 3:13

Lately, I have been blaming other people for my misery. People not even involved in my struggles are suddenly in my way or the cause of trouble. I feel frustrated by those who go about life without problems right now. I realize I cannot see what they struggle with, but in my desire to find reasons for my hurt, I want to blame other people.

Lord, where there are real grievances, please help me forgive the person and to see beyond the situation. May I never use another person as a reason to not follow Your lead.

Putting the Past to Rest

Brothers, I do not consider myself yet to have taken hold of it. But one thing I do: Forgetting what is behind and straining toward what is ahead, I press on toward the goal to win the prize for which God has called me heavenward in Christ Jesus.

PHILIPPIANS 3:13-14

I flip through my history as though I am looking at a photo album of past mistakes. I take the images out, one by one, and I scrutinize everything about the moment. *What was I thinking? How could I? How was I to know? I was so stupid. I should never have.* It is an endless cycle of guilt, such a waste of energy.

I pray to forget what is behind me so that I can press on toward the goal. You have a purpose for my life. When I spend my time reflecting on the past, I am avoiding the future. Do not let me waste another day focused on regrets.

Send Me

Then I heard the voice of the Lord saying, "Whom shall I send? And who will go for us?" And I said, "Here am I. Send me!"

ISAIAH 6:8

No more hiding—I have tried that in the past, and my problems still find me. When will I learn that it is better to stand up at the beginning and ask You to send me out into my future, Your will, and my life? I want to have the courage to say, "Send me" to You, Lord. When You are seeking hearts that long to abide by Your Word and to trust Your guidance, I want to be counted faithful.

I could hide forever. I could make up reasons why I do not want to move forward and trust Your will, but no more. Send me, Lord. Here I am.

Protection

Called by Name

The watchman opens the gate for him, and the sheep listen to his voice. He calls his own sheep by name and leads them out. When he has brought out all his own, he goes on ahead of them, and his sheep follow him because they know his voice.

JOHN 10:3-4

I listen for Your voice, God. I believe You are my Shepherd and that You stand here with me in the rain, the storm, the winds, and You call me by name. So much has happened that there are times I think I have forgotten the sound of Your voice. But I do not need to rely on my faulty memory, because my heart will not forget the tone, the inflection, and the leading of Your voice.

You call me by name, and I move toward Your voice. I am exhausted, lost, and far from shelter until I return to Your side. And here, again by Your strength, I am protected. I am home.

I Am Blessed

Blessed are those who are persecuted because of righteousness, for theirs is the kingdom of heaven.

MATTHEW 5:10

Along this road, I have encountered many who seem to work against me, Lord. I have tried to stand up for what is right, what I believe, how I am blessed even in the midst of strife. My resolve seems to dissolve when people disagree or do not support me in the way that I need. Help me understand and truly believe that I do not need approval from other people. And if their offers fall short or come with stipulations, I need not worry.

Today my needs are met by You. And when time has visited and left, and my days are no longer to be spent in the world, I will be blessed to be in the presence of the One who filled my needs throughout the journey.

The Fortress of Knowledge

Then you will understand what is right and just and fair—every good path. For wisdom will enter your heart, and knowledge will be pleasant to your soul. Discretion will protect you, and understanding will guard you.

PROVERBS 2:9-11

Because my view of life has changed, deepened because of my hurts, I find that I am understanding more about You and the value of life. Awareness does not deepen the wounds in the way I had feared. Understanding does reveal places of hurt that I had not even known existed. But on the heels of understanding, You offer wisdom and knowledge which create a fortress around my heart.

Within that fortress, my heart and spirit have a chance for restoration. You created knowledge to be a part of Your plan for my healing, Lord. No pain can match the wisdom and leading of Your love.

My Refuge

Guard my life and rescue me; let me not be put to shame, for I take refuge in you.

PSALM 25:20

I watch the news and see images of modern refugees. The thought of fighting for survival is overwhelming. I know my situation does not compare to that of these families, yet there is a sense of connection with them as I experience pain and desperation of my own. The world is not my savior, nor my restorer.

When I leave the world's offerings and ask You to guard my moves and rescue me from a fallen life, I come to You as a refugee. Bring me into the borders of Your grace, Lord.

Love

Because You Are Good

Answer me, O LORD, out of the goodness of your love; in your great mercy turn to me.

PSALM 69:16

Because You are good.

Because You are the Source of mercy that all the world longs for.

Because You are my Lord, Redeemer, and Creator.

Because You see my pain and know my deepest fear.

Because Your peace is a balm for my troubled soul.

Because You have been with me before I was born.

Because Your eyes see through my efforts to save myself.

Because You brought light to my darkest hour.

Because You are love,

You answer my plea for mercy.

Beyond a Doubt

*Know therefore that the LORD your God is God; he
is the faithful God, keeping his covenant of love to a
thousand generations of those who love him and
keep his commands.*

DEUTERONOMY 7:9

There have been times recently that I have ques-
tioned who You are in my life, Lord. I wonder how I can
feel this way when I am a person of faith. I have even
said You were unfair or unjust or unfaithful. But I know
that I am like an adulterous woman who blames
another for her indiscretion. I have turned from You
when I needed You most.

Only now can I remove the blinders of my self-
thinking and see that You are faithful, and have been all
along. I notice signs of Your love and care all about me.
For generations You have been a God of love to Your
people. May my life become one of these stories of
covenant and faith.

Bring On the Compassion

May your unfailing love be my comfort, according to your promise to your servant. Let your compassion come to me that I may live, for your law is my delight.

PSALM 119:76-77

Today I need it more than yesterday. I feel my hopefulness slipping away. A few missteps and moments of doubt now lead me to Your feet, requesting an extra dose of compassion. I know I asked just last week, but I am on a roll...or a downward spiral. I cling to the hope of Your unfailing love. Let this be my comfort when my circumstances feel cold and without reprieve.

So I ask once more, because You extend grace that is not of temporal human standards, but of eternity. Bring on the compassion, Lord.

Remember Me

Remember, O LORD, your great mercy and love, for they are from of old. Remember not the sins of my youth and my rebellious ways; according to your love remember me, for you are good, O Lord.

PSALM 25:6-7

Remember me with kindness, Lord. See me through the lens of forgiveness that blurs my past sins and my times of rebellion with the wash of Your grace. My wrongdoings are transformed by my Creator's eye for renewal. Remember me as I was that day I first met You...unsure of myself but certain of You and Your love. Forgive me when I can only recall my transgressions and not the times of renewal, Lord.

I have walked in Your ways. I have loved other people with Your compassion. By Your grace, I am not defined by the mistakes that litter my past. I am a new creation. Help me and remember me with kindness.

Peace

Deaf Ears

The LORD has heard my cry for mercy; the LORD accepts my prayer.

PSALM 6:9

They are all about me—deaf ears. My friends, my family, the strangers I try to connect with from my place of brokenness—nobody hears my cries. And yet each plea, each request for kindness or effort seems so very loud in my own head, my own heart. After each effort, I found myself more hurt. Can I really be this invisible?

As I desperately searched for someone to see me fully, care deeply, my own spirit reminded me to return to You. My words might be messy, my request in need of refinement, but Your ears are always open to my needs. I cry for the first time out of a sense of peace. I do not need to keep searching. Thank You, Lord. To be heard is transforming.

The Way of Peace

Do not repay anyone evil for evil. Be careful to do what is right in the eyes of everybody. If it is possible, as far as it depends on you, live at peace with everyone.

ROMANS 12:17-18

With conflict in my life, there are times that I turn from a way of peace and feed the fire of tension. I offer You my harsh words and my need for personal justice, Lord. Before I extend them to another of Your children or turn judgment toward myself, give me peace.

Strengthen my steps today. Fortify my sense of love. Help me see myself as a vessel that takes in Your love and funnels it to other people. When my humanity desires to pursue unkind actions and responses, may I turn to Your Word, Your message, and be redirected to the way of peace.

Inner Storms

He got up, rebuked the wind and said to the waves,
"Quiet! Be still!" Then the wind died down and it
was completely calm. He said to his disciples, "Why
are you so afraid? Do you still have no faith?"

MARK 4:39-40

God, I am afraid of the inner storm that brews deep
within my soul, too close to the shore of my daily life.
The rough waters could destroy all that I care about.
Just like Your disciples, I watch You calm the seas, and
yet I still do not fully believe that Your power can hold
me up or subside the torrents in my spirit.

I reveal my rage to You, Lord. I see You rebuke my
wild emotions. And as peace replaces the jagged edge of
leftover pain, I believe that You, Lord, will hold me up.

They Are Yours

Blessed are the peacemakers, for they will be called sons of God.

MATTHEW 5:9

Thank You, Lord, for those You call Your sons and daughters who are peacemakers in this world of angst, fear, and self-protection. I hope to be such a person. I see how this time of personal struggle is shaping me to be a peacemaker. My heart and eyes have been opened to how much I and all people need Your peace in this earthly journey. Your peace is the foundation from which we can reach for the heavens. It is the source that lets us love when we feel empty, uncertain, or wronged.

I believe my hurts have allowed me a deeper sensitivity to the needs of other people. Please direct me to use this gift.

Meaning

Anchored in Purpose

We must pay more careful attention, therefore, to what we have heard, so that we do not drift away.

HEBREWS 2:1

Give me a perceptive mind, wide eyes, and patience to take in the lessons You have for me during this time. I get lost in my thoughts and worries, but I feel the pull of Your will bringing me out of this despair. You have a reason for my life.

I do not want to be drifting away from Your words of guidance and direction. I pray to be anchored in Your truth and purpose so that I might discover the meaning of each day, trial, and victory that is part of my journey.

Your Hold on My Life

Not that I have already obtained all this, or have already been made perfect, but I press on to take hold of that for which Christ Jesus took hold of me.

PHILIPPIANS 3:12

Your hands shaped the fabric of my soul and body. Before I took my first steps, You saw my last ones. And You know the condition of every step in between. As I move forward, may my steps become stronger, bolder, and more willing to deviate from my own way in order to follow Your perfect will.

When I found You, Lord, Your love took hold of me. It was the day my life was given meaning. I hold on to that same sense of hope and significance today.

The Meaning of It All

For everything that was written in the past was written to teach us, so that through endurance and the encouragement of the Scriptures we might have hope.

ROMANS 15:4

Thank goodness I was not asked ahead of time if I would accept the burdens that are in my life right now. God, I know what I would have said. But even though I did not have advance knowledge of what to expect, I do have Your knowledge to carry me through each day. Your words, communicated through obedient servants over time, now serve to build me up and restore my strength.

My chance to say no would have eliminated my opportunity to say yes—yes to learning to trust You, yes to enduring the dark to reach the light, and yes to receiving the hope that gives all my days meaning.

Sentimental Value

*Jesus answered, "If you want to be perfect, go, sell
your possessions and give to the poor, and you will
have treasure in heaven. Then come, follow me."
When the young man heard this, he went away sad,
because he had great wealth.*

MATTHEW 19:21-22

When I read that it is difficult for a rich man to get
to heaven, I always breathe a little easier. I am not
wealthy, so this appears to be a complication far removed from me. Yet, how many items, people, and
situations do I grip because they hold great senti-
mental value to me. I cannot imagine my life without
these things. They are my riches that I place between
me and heaven.

Then You say to give them over, to be willing to sacrifice that which has great meaning and come follow
You. Lord, help me to let go of these things. I pray I will
not face a time of sorrow by only wanting to follow after
possessions or preferences. I want to follow You.

Reaching

Reaching for Dreams

*May he give you the desire of your heart and make
all your plans succeed. We will shout for joy when
you are victorious and will lift up our banners in
the name of our God.*

PSALM 20:4-5

Lord, do not let me stop reaching for the dreams I
have been given. While my health, thoughts, and
energy seem to be spent on survival right now, I have
faith in the dreams of old. You planted them deep in my
being so that through the storm of distraction, these
dreams are protected.

The success I envision does not involve wealth or
power. My plan for success requires only that I uncover
my preserved dreams and give You the glory when they
are restored and realized.

Hear My Prayer

You are forgiving and good, O Lord, abounding in love to all who call to you. Hear my prayer, O LORD; listen to my cry for mercy. In the day of my trouble I will call to you, for you will answer me.

PSALM 86:5-7

I have never been one to ask for help. You know my stubbornness, Lord. You have witnessed my tight lips when I should have been asking another person for assistance, or prayer, or comfort. Do not let me fall under this spirit of isolation and independence, Lord. If others have let me down, and that is why I go it alone, release me from this restriction.

Your love anoints the one who calls out for Your mercy. My day of trouble is upon me, and I part my lips to pray out loud to You. Hear my prayer, Lord.

Touching the Garment

*When she heard about Jesus, she came up behind
him in the crowd and touched his cloak, because she
thought, "If I just touch his clothes, I will be healed."
Immediately her bleeding stopped and she felt in
her body that she was freed from her suffering.…
Then the woman, knowing what had happened to
her, came and fell at his feet and, trembling with
fear, told him the whole truth. He said to her,
"Daughter, your faith has healed you. Go in peace
and be freed from your suffering."*

MARK 5:27-29, 33-34

I have learned to fear the consequences of believing,
of asking for what I need, of reaching out to touch the
power of love. I learn this fear from my relationships
with fallible people, not from my communion with You.
Teach me to release those past hurts so that I can touch,
without fear, the hem of Your garment and believe in a
faith that heals.

You call me "Child" because You are Abba, Father.
You see my steps of faith and do not judge them, but
call them worthy of healing because You love me.

Grasping for a Miracle

*Moses answered, "What if they do not believe me or
listen to me and say, 'The LORD did not appear to you'?"
Then the LORD said to him, "What is that in your hand?"
"A staff," he replied. The LORD said, "Throw it on the
ground." Moses threw it on the ground and it became a
snake, and he ran from it. Then the LORD said to him,
"Reach out your hand and take it by the tail." So Moses
reached out and took hold of the snake and it turned
back into a staff in his hand. "This," said the LORD, "is so
that they may believe that the LORD, the God of their
fathers—the God of Abraham, the God of Isaac and the
God of Jacob—has appeared to you."*

EXODUS 4:1-5

Moses was so afraid that nobody would believe his
authority had come from You, Lord. I am like that too.
I do not speak up about the good things You will do in
my life because I fear other people will doubt me.
Maybe I question Your power as well. I want to believe
with all my heart, Lord.

May I reach out and take the difficult situation by
the tail so You can transform my trial into a symbol of
hope and authority. Let my miracle say to everyone that
You are in control of my life. And may they believe
because of it.

Acceptance

Lead Me

By faith Abraham, when called to go to a place he would later receive as his inheritance, obeyed and went, even though he did not know where he was going.

HEBREWS 11:8

Anyone watching me must surely know that I do not know where I am going. Nevertheless, I do accept that I am going forward in Your will and with the blessing of Your leading.

I have to shrug my shoulders when people ask me why I remain strong during times of loss or frustration. I can only explain my love for You and my unwavering belief that my inheritance in You is eternity. And when compared to that sure thing in my future, today's uncertainty has no power over my faith.

The Challenge

He held fast to the LORD and did not cease to follow him; he kept the commands the LORD had given Moses. And the LORD was with him; he was successful in whatever he undertook.

2 KINGS 18:6-7

I accept the challenge of continuing to follow where You direct my life, Lord. When I cannot understand the why or how of difficult moments, I can return to a place of obedience and commitment. I can keep Your commands because You have authority over my life. I do not do this because I am told to do so. I am able to abide by Your law because of the gift of Your grace.

Success is the result of holding fast to Your strength. I could not get from here to there on my own. You are the God of Moses, and I, too, follow where You lead me.

Receiving Gifts

Moreover, when God gives any man wealth and possessions, and enables him to enjoy them, to accept his lot and be happy in his work—this is a gift of God. He seldom reflects on the days of his life, because God keeps him occupied with gladness of heart.

ECCLESIASTES 5:19-20

As much as I shy away from asking for help, God, I also shy away from receiving gifts, even those that come from Your hands and are meant for my specific needs. Do I not feel worthy? Have I not learned anything from the story of Christ's love and sacrifice? If I were to wait until I was worthy of the gifts that flow from Your heart, I would never be able to accept them.

If trouble pushes me to unhappiness or toward a desire to earn the hope of heaven, my hands will be closed and unable to receive Your blessing. Give me a heart that is occupied by gladness and peace so that I am always ready and willing to accept the goodness that is born of Your grace.

Humble Words

Accept, O LORD, the willing praise of my mouth, and teach me your laws. Though I constantly take my life in my hands, I will not forget your law.

PSALM 119:108-109

Though this mouth of mine is used to express doubt, hurt, or confusion about my life right now, Lord, please accept the words of praise that also fall from these trembling lips. I do not mean to be double-minded. I am trying to find my way to Your will and teachings. My choices place my life at risk at times. Reveal to me Your laws that govern my steps and protect me from destruction.

My praise is sincere. Through these tears, my shouts of joy come from a spirit of worship. This is my faith in the wonders of Your will that I have not yet witnessed.

Giving and Receiving

What Do You Say?

*By faith Abel offered God a better sacrifice than
Cain did. By faith he was commended as a righteous man, when God spoke well of his offerings.*

HEBREWS 11:4

God, I give to You my burdens today. I have some
messes in my life. My collection of emotions is covered
with dirt, and many pieces are chipped, imperfect.
These days, it seems this is all I have to offer anyone.
But I know that as I hand You each of these troubles,
stains, and seemingly worthless portions of a soul, You
make them splendid and shiny.

What will You say when I turn over what is in my
heart today, when I offer You all that is my life, even
though it is not much of anything—at least not yet? I
pray You speak well of these bits of my life, Lord. Speak
them into a miracle of transformation.

It Ain't Much

He also saw a poor widow put in two very small copper coins. "I tell you the truth," he said, "this poor widow has put in more than all the others. All these people gave their gifts out of their wealth; but she out of her poverty put in all she had to live on."

LUKE 21:2-4

I keep going back to the story of the poor widow. I feel I am her: poor in spirit, poor in energy, poor in hope right now. Yet I fumble in my pockets and look in my change jar and find a few last pennies to give to You. I walk past people who seem to have their act together and who pull out nice, crisp bills or a checkbook. I keep walking because You are there in front of me.

I can hear You saying not to look at what pours from the pockets and hearts of these men, because what I have to give is enough. It ain't much. It barely makes a noise as I release it to the pile. But somehow I know it adds up to greatness here on the altar of eternity.

By Any Standards

You see, at just the right time, when we were still
powerless, Christ died for the ungodly. Very rarely
will anyone die for a righteous man, though for a
good man someone might possibly dare to die. But
God demonstrates his own love for us in this: While
we were still sinners, Christ died for us.

ROMANS 5:6-8

To die for someone is beyond sacrifice. I can think
of people in my life that I would give my life for, but
what if You threw me in a situation where I had to stand
in the place of a killer, a rapist, a person who hurt one
of those people I would give my life for? By any standards, that would be absurd, unexpected, completely
not the normal thing to do. I could decline and say,
"Who would do such a thing?"

You would.

And while this entire thought is hypothetical on my
end, it is not hypothetical to You. I am that one who is
capable of hurting the people You cared enough to die
for. Yet, You died for me. By any standards, Lord, You
are my Savior.

Give Me All That You Have

For you know the grace of our Lord Jesus Christ, that though he was rich, yet for your sakes he became poor, so that you through his poverty might become rich.

2 CORINTHIANS 8:9

I face a time of sacrifice and loss. I seem to be forced or called to give up those things I took for granted: security, happiness, stability, and certainty, to name a few. I never considered myself rich, but I had things I could count on, things I could control. Now I must face a poverty that leads me back to my knees, begging for all that You are and have.

Lord, You gave up great wealth and power and instead, took a vow of poverty and covenant with those in Your charge. From this poverty, You offer me new riches: security, peace, certainty, and a sure faith in You.

Wholeness

Made by God

Through him all things were made; without him nothing was made that has been made. In him was life, and that life was the light of men. The light shines in the darkness, but the darkness has not understood it.

JOHN 1:3-5

You make whole creations. You made my heart, my life, and my faith. Within the circle of Your love and care, these pieces of me are whole, Lord. I feel pangs, like parts of my faith are being removed or threatened. I hold my side, as if the light is going to pour out of me and never return. Some days I lie down on my couch and hug a pillow to keep my heart from moving and breaking.

In my fragile state of being, I know You gather up this creation that You made and bathe me in light and life. Slowly I will quit checking for holes and leaks in my spirit. Slowly I will believe You made a whole and perfect vessel.

The Whole Story

*I will turn their mourning into gladness; I will give
them comfort and joy instead of sorrow.*

JEREMIAH 31:13

If I could look forward in time, I would see this
burden being lifted. I would understand that this pang
of hurt would be reshaped into joy and wisdom. I
would witness Your hand lifting me up above my circumstances. Why do I get so focused on this chapter of
my life that I refuse to consider the whole story?

I know that, when I lean on my faith, I give myself
a chance to believe in what comes next. I want to
believe that mourning turns to gladness if I just keep
living this life and reading Your Word for my life. The
joy of this thought, even right now, is that I want to
keep pushing forward. I cannot wait to read about my
brokenness turning to wholeness in this story You are
telling through me.

Usher Me In

But you, dear friends, build yourselves up in your most holy faith and pray in the Holy Spirit. Keep yourselves in God's love as you wait for the mercy of our Lord Jesus Christ to bring you to eternal life.

JUDE 20-21

Teach me to pray in the Holy Spirit, Lord. I have started to pray in my own way, from my own starving state of being. Somewhere I started to turn back to my need for power over my own life and it has lessened my prayers. They are mere shadows of the passionate praises and cries I shouted toward heaven at the beginning of this journey.

My numbness lets me distance myself from the leading of the Spirit. Do not let me deny this power in my life, Lord. My prayers are worthless until I allow myself to stay in Your love and wait, with belief, for Your mercy. Usher me into Your presence, Lord. I pray to be made whole.

Renewal of Spirit

Create in me a pure heart, O God, and renew a stead-fast spirit within me.

PSALM 51:10

Today's culture has completely lost sight of Your art of renewal. We upgrade, replace, toss out, give away, or tear apart and dispose of many things in our lives. Few people take the time to restore things in the way that You tend to our hearts.

Yet, Lord, You can take this very weary child and see a life worthy of attention. You do not say my spirit is not worth keeping. You do not try to pawn my troubles off on someone else. You do not consider removing pieces and turning me into some unrecognizable "other" thing. You see the value and purpose of my spirit. And as You cover me in grace, You restore my spirit to such a state of shine and luster that I can see my faith reflected in its surface.

Perspective

Considering My Options

*Consider it pure joy, my brothers, whenever you
face trials of many kinds, because you know that
the testing of your faith develops perseverance.*

JAMES 1:2-3

When I peruse a menu, I like to look at all my
options. I consider how the chicken teriyaki could
enrich my life (or at least my dining experience) compared to the stir-fried vegetables over rice noodles. So
why do I refuse to look at other ways of viewing my
situation, Lord? I go straight for what I know: regret,
blame, sorrow, and forget that there is a "lite" side of
the menu.

Help me to consider my trials with a sense of joy.
Deepen my understanding of how life works so that I
can rejoice in this testing of my faith. I want to be one
who perseveres. I want to consider how choosing joy
could enrich my life and my faith experience.

It Is What It Is

Therefore, prepare your minds for action; be self-controlled; set your hope fully on the grace to be given you when Jesus Christ is revealed.

1 PETER 1:13

My friend has a personal trainer. It is a way to get motivated to do the work when this person might rather go eat popcorn and watch a movie. Lately, I have not felt very motivated to do the work I need to for the sake of my faith. Every time I turn around, there is more work to do: a weakness that needs to be strengthened, a muscle of spiritual proportion that should be exercised with diligence.

May I see this trial as my personal trainer. Whether I wanted one or not, this trial is helping me do the work I have put off for too long. This struggle is preparing my mind for action. This working out of my emotions is giving me an enduring hope.

Looking Back

Look to the LORD and his strength; seek his face always. Remember the wonders he has done.

1 CHRONICLES 16:11-12

To get through this time, I place a lot of hope in my future, the part of my life I have not yet experienced. It becomes a treasure chest of possible change, healing, and best of all, it becomes the "anywhere but here" that I need to cling to. But the other day, someone reminded me of an experience I have gone through, one in which I relied daily on Your grace and direction.

Lord, help me to turn toward my past in this time of trial. I have been trying to scan the future for so long, to mine a bit of hope, that I forgot the wealth of hope behind me. Thank You for leading me through yesterday, Lord. Your faithfulness speaks to me today.

No False Motives

But the wisdom that comes from heaven is first of all pure; then peace-loving, considerate, submissive, full of mercy and good fruit, impartial and sincere.

JAMES 3:17

I have been tossing about faulty wisdom lately, Lord. I say things to myself or other people about my pain that I do not believe. They are dangerous, flippant references to how life works, how You work in these times. My perspective is tainted by my own wishes and objectives. Even as I pray this, I am formulating another idea of how my life should turn out.

God, give me Your perspective, Your wisdom, Your words so that the fruit of my speech and deeds becomes sweet in Your purpose, not bitter in my own. Give me holy motives that turn me to You and Your truth at all times.

Belief

Never Failing

You know with all your heart and soul that not one of all the good promises the LORD your God gave you has failed. Every promise has been fulfilled; not one has failed.

JOSHUA 23:14

I can read off a list of mistakes, broken promises, and unfulfilled expectations, but this list only reflects my own side of our relationship, Lord. I see Your faithfulness in every turn of my life. I struggle to remember that during my darker days or times like now, when I feel I am juggling too many responsibilities and everyone else is letting me down.

So when I am ready to complain that there is nowhere to turn, that there is nothing to believe in anymore, remind me, Lord, that You are a God who keeps His Word…to me, to my life, to this faith journey I am on.

One More Time

Though the doors were locked, Jesus came and stood among them and said, "Peace be with you!" Then he said to Thomas, "Put your finger here; see my hands. Reach out your hand and put it into my side. Stop doubting and believe." Thomas said to him, "My Lord and my God!"

JOHN 20:26-28

I have asked to do this a few times in my past, but I am most certain that this time is the most crucial to my faith, Lord. Please, can I look at the holes in Your hands one more time? Can I approach You as Thomas did, filled with doubt and questions and uncertainty? It is not so much that I am on a quest for proof. I just need assurance. I need You to calm me once again with Your peace.

And I need You to call me on this behavior and say, "Stop doubting and believe." I am ready to get back to all that You have for me in this life, Lord. But can I look, just one more time?

Just As I Believe

Then Jesus said to the centurion, "Go! It will be done just as you believed it would." And his servant was healed at that very hour.

MATTHEW 8:13

Lord, You give me belief, and then honor that belief with miracles every day. It is only when I waiver, when I start relying on myself or other people too much that Your touch begins to fade. Our relationship involves both of us, and I do not always hold up my part.

Today I need You so badly. I come to You with deep, abiding faith. I am in my last hour of strength for this journey, Lord. I have waited too long to give myself over to disbelief. You take my hand and lead me to a higher place where hope rushes about me and I am revived.

Morning 'Til Night

Show me your ways, O LORD, teach me your paths;
guide me in your truth and teach me, for you are
God my Savior, and my hope is in you all day long.

PSALM 25:4-5

I awaken to Your mercies, Lord. I know that I do not get out of bed and go to work without the sustaining power of Your love. While my mind spins with frustrations and possible worst-case scenarios for my life, You calm my emotions and let me focus on the job before me. You even help me see the needs of other people in the midst of my own need.

I come home feeling I have actually accomplished something—an amazing feeling that curbs my feelings of going nowhere in my time of trial. Some nights I cannot sleep, yet even then You are there to comfort me and teach me patience. Each day, morning 'til night, is such a gift when I give it over to You, Lord.

Joy

Because of Hope

Be joyful in hope, patient in affliction, faithful in prayer. Share with God's people who are in need. Practice hospitality.

ROMANS 12:12-13

Because my faith tells me that tomorrow will be different, I have hope. Because I have this hope in my heart, I have joy. My difficulties are not fading, nor are they being removed from my responsibilities right now, but I have joy.

When I feel I have nothing to give, You call me to extend Your love to other people, and in that act of obedience I find joy. How You are able to lift my spirit out of the depths of despair, Lord, is the greatest mystery and delight of my faith. Thank You, Lord.

Crossing Over

*Restore to me the joy of your salvation and grant
me a willing spirit, to sustain me.*

PSALM 51:12

I have been a reluctant child of Yours lately. I am
dragging my feet and my spirit right along with 'em.
God, I really want to have a willing spirit. I want to
draw from Your well of salvation and sip of Your mercy
and joy. I want to experience this renewal now. I just
need help crossing over from this place of apathy to the
place of belief.

Help me to watch for Your provision. Turn my feet
toward Your heart. I want to walk to You, crawl to
You—whatever it takes to cross over that line I have created that separates me from Your joy.

Way to Joy

Finally, brothers, whatever is true, whatever is noble, whatever is right, whatever is pure, whatever is lovely, whatever is admirable—if anything is excellent or praiseworthy—think about such things.

PHILIPPIANS 4:8

I know the way to joy. I watch other people about me also go through their struggles, and they do not know that the way of joy exists, let alone how to get there. You give me what I need to persevere and receive the joy of eternity. I might want to gather troubles, trip over them, shove them aside, and bring them out again, but You tell me to let go of such things and turn my attention to whatever is true, noble, right, pure, lovely, admirable, excellent, and praiseworthy.

Just repeating that list, Lord, reminds me of the goodness in my life and all around me. Through the rubble of destruction, Lord, Your words and Your truth carve out the way to joy.

Something About Today

This day is sacred to our Lord. Do not grieve, for the joy of the LORD is your strength.

NEHEMIAH 8:10

I start out the day with steps that are heavy with grief. I feel the pressure of life on my shoulders and begin to cave toward the sidewalk. My countenance is drawn and expressionless. I see how other people respond to me and am taken aback by the reflection of my sadness in their eyes. Then, out of nowhere and straight from Your hand, a single perfect leaf rushes past my line of vision. I watch it float, taking its time. It does not rush to the ground with the weight of burdens.

It is as if I can see Your hand cradling this symbol of a new season. You let it glide in the sky, and then You gently guide it to safety. The wind on my back becomes Your gentle hand, and I know that today is sacred. It is a day in which my journey is guided to safety by Your strength and will. I give myself over to this with great relief.

Character

The Best Part

May integrity and uprightness protect me, because my hope is in you.

PSALM 25:21

Lord, is the best part of me showing right now? Is my focus so much on my problems that I do not allow my godly character to make an appearance? I worry that my complaining has become my only communication, that my sighs and tears have become the only evidence that I am alive.

May my hope in You be the force which moves me to interact with people. May my upright life and character be honorable and evident in all that I do and say. Your hope is the best part of me and of this time in my life. May it shine.

Chitchat

The wise in heart accept commands, but a chattering fool comes to ruin.

PROVERBS 10:8

I overdid it, Lord. Once my mouth opened up, it was useless. Everything in me poured out: the hurt, the questions, the doubting, the anger. I was not paying attention to the person I was talking to, and I ignored this individual's need for consolation, not commiseration. I know what this is like. I have come to You so many times after someone has done the same to me.

"This is my heart, be careful with it." This is what we require of one another, yet we are foolish. We turn the situation into a stage for our woeful performance. I pray to become wise in such matters, Lord.

No Substitute

An honest answer is like a kiss on the lips.

PROVERBS 24:26

Meaningful...full of promise...trusting...vulnerable...appreciated...remembered. Honesty is such a powerful way to express love to another person...Your love. It becomes a kiss on the lips to someone in need of affection and tenderness.

When I am tempted to offer someone an answer that is less than truthful about my circumstances, Lord, help me to see how my honesty in that moment could be a gift for myself and the other person. Let me release my pride and be willing to share the hard stuff when I feel led. Just when I want to call my hardship a jagged rock, an open wound, You are ready to turn it into a beautiful gem, a sweet kiss.

Discovery

Are You Talking to Me?

A voice of one calling in the desert, "Prepare the way for the Lord, make straight paths for him."

LUKE 3:4

What a wonderful day...the day I discovered that You were talking to me. At first You sounded like a wise friend. The next day You sounded like my pastor. Just yesterday You were the voice of a stranger who shared from her experience in life. Lord, through these people, I am discovering Your voice and all its mercy.

Sometimes it takes me awhile to understand the message. Your written Word guides me, and my heart understands what it is You are telling me. Only now can I heed the words of John to prepare the way for the Lord. I am learning to prepare the way for the Savior of my heart to rule my life. I am finally listening.

You Can Do That?

*Now to each one the manifestation of the Spirit is
given for the common good. To one there is given
through the Spirit the message of wisdom, to another
the message of knowledge by means of the same
Spirit, to another faith by the same Spirit.*

1 CORINTHIANS 12:7-9

I am amazed how You bring people together for a
reason. At first I connect with people and feel a sense of
camaraderie, often because of similarities—one thing
that might bond us. Over time or varying circumstances, I begin to notice the differences, and how well
we complement one another.

You are a God of so many mysteries. The way You
work in and through people is mighty. Help me discover the beauty of the differences that I witness in
other people. I long to see what You see in them and to
understand how we are part of one another's journey.

Twist of Fate

The women said to Naomi: "Praise be to the LORD, who this day has not left you without a kinsman-redeemer. May he become famous throughout Israel! He will renew your life and sustain you in your old age."

RUTH 4:14-15

I am surprised by the new direction of my life, Lord. Even though the point of change is rocky, I do see the fruit of this labor. I understand that other people will look at my life and be able to see Your touch of renewal and authority. Who else but You could direct this course of events and have it lead to anything wonderful?

I must praise You with each step because I hold fast to Your ways in honor of Your faithfulness. You have not left me without a redeemer. You have not left me standing alone at this juncture. I take the next steps without worry, but with eagerness to see even this hardship through to Your end.

Limitations

Jesus looked at them and said, "With man this is impossible, but with God all things are possible."

MATTHEW 19:26

My life, when it seemed to be under my control, was very limited. No wonder the unbreakable, insurmountable walls of difficulty were being built along my path faster than I could create detours. I had no vision, no wisdom, no power.

Only with You is it possible to go beyond my personal limitations. Only with Your strength can I defeat the warriors or storm the castles that stand between me and Your plan for my journey. My true destination was impossible in the days of old. I am so thankful I discovered how limited my view of life was at that time. May I see only the wonders ahead…the wonders that can be achieved only with You as my God.

Changing Course

New Things Right Around the Corner

See, I am doing a new thing! Now it springs up; do you not perceive it? I am making a way in the desert and streams in the wasteland.

ISAIAH 43:19

No. No, Lord, I did not see a new thing coming my way. Nor was I always believing that there would be something redeeming in the days ahead. But You can lead Your people through the desert. You can drop manna from heaven. And You can make streams in the wasteland that was my life.

How fitting that as my faith in You is restored, so is the clarity of the path before me. All the signs point to a new and wonderful way. The strength that had gone from my muscles and my mind is now back. Redemption and wholeness are just up ahead.

What I Need

"For I know the plans I have for you," declares the
LORD, "plans to prosper you and not to harm you,
plans to give you hope and a future."

JEREMIAH 29:11

I need to be heard right now, Lord. My weaknesses are revealed to You, even as I hide them from other people. My prayers are heard by You, even though they barely rise from my spirit. You are changing me into a new creation because You know me so well and care that I find the plan with my name on it.

There is hope and a future on this new course. My days of wandering the familiar roads of fear or pain will give way to a future of sight-seeing vast new countries of change and potential. Even before I called out to You, the path for me to survive and prosper was being paved with Your mercy.

I Am Learning

Who is wise? He will realize these things. Who is discerning? He will understand them. The ways of the LORD are right; the righteous walk in them, but the rebellious stumble in them.

HOSEA 14:9

I am growing and learning through You—the great I Am. My discernment is granted from heaven. Wisdom is bestowed upon my life with the scepter of Your grace. My new course is that of a righteous person. I walk blamelessly and with honor because I am a servant of the King of kings.

At the beginning of this journey, I did not have these claims to make. It is only through Your goodness that I have made it thus far and have a future to believe in. I am understanding more about faith's might each day. My rebellious spirit has been replaced by a willing and eager heart. Lead me toward what is right and what is good.

Searching for Joy

*Direct me in the path of your commands, for there
I find delight. Turn my heart toward your statutes
and not toward selfish gain.*

PSALM 119:35-36

Direct me toward good times, Lord. However You work…however prayer works…I have to ask for this desire of my heart right now. My eyes are tired of crying. My muscles ache from too many days of tension. I find myself waiting for more pain to come my way.

So direct me in the path of Your ways. Lead me to brighter times. Turn my heart toward the faith lessons You have for me so that I might rejoice when I arrive, when I turn that corner and face delight, pleasure, laughter that releases the ache that has resided for too long in my heart. My search for joy begins with this prayer. Point me in the right direction.

Once Again

O Lord, the God who saves me, day and night I cry out before you. May my prayer come before you; turn your ear to my cry.

PSALM 88:1-2

Faithfully You have brought me through another day. Your mercy flows day and night to keep me going. I pray to serve You well tomorrow. Tonight I will not worry. My thoughts will not become a list of regrets or fears. As the sky darkens, I am able to offer up my prayers to You, and You turn Your ear to my cry.

Thank You, Lord, for not releasing me to my sorrow this evening. Your tight hold on my heart keeps me from trembling. Your embrace preserves my hope.

And once again, You save me.

Other Inspiring Titles
in the One-Minute Prayers™ Series

ONE-MINUTE PRAYERS™
This collection of simple, heartfelt prayers and Scriptures is designed to serve the pace and needs of everyday life. Offering renewal, this prayer journey encourages readers to experience fellowship with God during busy times.

ONE-MINUTE PRAYERS™ FOR BUSY MOMS
Designed to serve the pace and needs of everyday life, these simple prayers and inspirational verses are available when needed most. A mother's minute in prayer will free her to find refreshment in God's presence.

ONE-MINUTE PRAYERS™ FOR MEN
These themed, brief prayers draw men to the feet of Jesus where wisdom, direction, and guidance are offered. The format is ideal for businessmen, travelers, and men ready to develop the discipline of prayer.

ONE-MINUTE PRAYERS™ FOR WOMEN
Women who juggle schedules, responsibilities, and commitments will discover sacred moments of renewal among these brief prayers. They will experience the joy of meditation and learn to appreciate their gifts, release guilt, and embrace grace.

HARVEST HOUSE
PUBLISHERS